Arthur's Christmas Cookies

For my children
who know all about
clay cookies

I Can Read Book is a registered trademark of
Harper & Row, Publishers, Inc.

ARTHUR'S CHRISTMAS COOKIES   Copyright © 1972 by Lillian Hoban

Library of Congress Catalog Card Number: 72-76496
Trade Standard Book Number: 06-022367-7
Harpercrest Standard Book Number: 06-022368-5

An *I CAN READ* Book®

Arthur's
Christmas Cookies

Words and Pictures by

Lillian Hoban

Harper & Row, Publishers

It was the Saturday

before Christmas.

Mother and Father

were shopping.

Violet was making

a napkin-holder for Mother.

Arthur was watching the snow fall.

"I was making presents too,"
said Arthur. "I made
a wooden lamp for Father,
but it would not stand right.
I sawed off one side
to get it even.

But I sawed off too much.

Now it won't stand up at all."

"Why don't you *buy* presents?"

said Violet. "You could use

the money you were saving."

9

"Well, I only had
fifty-two cents,"
said Arthur.

"I bought two Slim Jims
for twenty cents
and a Big Buddy
for a nickel.

Then I was thirsty,
so I got a ten-cent soda.

After that I got
a Lola Finola Comic.

The last two pennies
fell out of my pocket.

They rolled into a crack

on the porch.

And now I can't get them out."

"Two cents is not enough
for presents anyway," said Violet.
"I know," said Arthur.
"I made Father a clay paperweight,"
said Violet. "I dried it
in my Bake-E-Z oven."
"Maybe I should try to make
something else," said Arthur.
"If you let me use
your Bake-E-Z oven,
I could bake some cookies."

"You don't know how

to make cookies," said Violet.

"Yes I do," said Arthur.

"We learned how

at cub scouts.

14

I can make Christmas cookies

for Mother and Father.

And I will make a special one

for you," said Arthur.

"All right," said Violet.

She ran to get her oven.

Arthur tied an apron

around his waist.

Then he got

the measuring cups,

the rolling pin,

and the cookie sheets.

"I do like baking cookies,"

said Arthur.

"You don't have to saw cookies.

You don't have to worry about

getting cookies to stand up.

And they are good to eat."

16

"Here is my Bake-E-Z oven,"
said Violet. "Remember,
you promised to make
a special cookie for me."
"I remember," said Arthur.

"I will make you

a special reindeer cookie."

"Arthur," called Norman.

"Come on out.

Let's have a snowball fight!"

"I can't come out," said Arthur.

"Why not?" asked Norman.

"I am baking cookies now,"
said Arthur.

"Can I come in?" asked Norman.

"Can I lick the bowl
and the scraper?"

"I am not making that kind,"
said Arthur.

"What kind are you making?"
asked Norman.

"I am making Christmas cookies.

The kind you roll out,"

said Arthur.

"I am making stars and angels

and bells for Mother,

and Christmas trees

and Santa Clauses

and reindeer for Father."

22

"You said you would make
a reindeer cookie for me,"
said Violet.

"I know," said Arthur.

"Let me help," said Violet.

"It is *my* oven."

"I will let you and Norman
get the flour and the sugar
and the butter," said Arthur.
"But I will make the cookies
by myself."

"All right," said Norman.
"Where is the flour?"

"It is next to the glass jar
of sugar," said Arthur.

Norman took down
the glass jar of flour
and the jar next to it.

"Now there is nothing

for me to do,"

said Violet.

"You can get the butter,"

said Arthur.

"All right," said Violet.

26

Arthur mixed the butter
and the sugar in a bowl.
He put the flour in too.
Then he added some water,
and patted the dough
into a large ball.

"Here is Wilma," said Violet.

"Can she watch you bake cookies?"

"My big sister bakes cookies,"
said Wilma. "She puts in
raisins and nuts.

And sometimes chocolate chips."

"I like that kind," said Norman.

"And I like oatmeal cookies
and ginger cookies
and the little sandwich cookies
with creme in between."

29

"Well," said Arthur.

"I am making plain sugar cookies."

"I like plain sugar cookies," said Norman.

"So do I," said Wilma.

"Move back, Violet," said Arthur.

"I can't roll out the dough without mashing your nose."

"It's Wilma," said Violet.

"She's pushing."

"You pushed me first," said Wilma, "and I'm pushing back."

"Watch out," yelled Arthur.

"Now look what you did!"

The ball of dough

fell on the floor.

It rolled under Norman's foot.

"It's still good,"

said Norman.

"Just a little dirty."

"That does it," said Arthur.

"All of you get out."

"Please," said Violet.

"We will be nice.

If you make us each

a special cookie,

I will make hot chocolate.

And we can have

a Before-Christmas Party."

"Can I have a Santa cookie?"

asked Norman.

"Me too?" said Wilma.

"All right," said Arthur.

"But no more pushing!"

Arthur rolled the dough flat.

He cut some cookies

for Mother and Father

and the special cookies too.

He made a Christmas tree

for himself.

Then he put the cookie sheets
in the Bake-E-Z oven.

"Now I will make hot chocolate," said Violet.

"Put some marshmallows in it," said Norman.

"My big sister puts whipped cream in hot chocolate," said Wilma.

"For Christmas parties, we stir it with candy canes."

"We don't have any candy canes," said Arthur.

"When will the cookies be done?" asked Violet.

They all looked inside the oven.

"The cookies don't look done,"
said Norman.
"They look just like they did
when you put them in."

"Well," said Arthur, "I think
they will be done
by the time
the hot chocolate is ready."
Arthur got the cups
and saucers and spoons.

Then he put a marshmallow
in the bottom of each cup.
Violet poured the hot chocolate,
and the marshmallows
floated to the top.

Arthur went to get the cookies.

"They look just like they did

before," he said.

"But they feel hard

when I push down on them.

So they must be done."

Arthur put the special Santas

and the special reindeer cookie

and the Christmas tree

on a plate.

"Now we can have our

Before-Christmas Party,"

said Violet.

"Norman's Santa fell on the floor,"

said Wilma. "But it did not break."

"How do you know it's

my Santa?" asked Norman.

"Because mine is still

on the plate," said Wilma.

44

"It's always mine that falls
on the floor," said Norman.

Norman took a bite of Santa's hat.

"What is the matter with Norman?"

said Violet.

"Norman's mouth is funny."

"You have to be careful

when you eat these cookies,"

said Norman.

"My loose front tooth came out.

But I never got a bite of cookie."

Arthur tried to bite into

his Christmas tree.

"Something is wrong," he said.

"This cookie is as hard as a rock."

"My sister's cookies are never hard,"

said Wilma. "I wish I had one now."

"I don't understand,"

said Arthur.

"I made the same dough

that we made at cub scouts."

"I am licking mine," said Violet.

"It tastes salty."

"These are salt cookies!"

said Norman.

"They *are* as hard as rocks."

Arthur looked at his cookies.

Then he looked at Norman.

Norman said, "I think I gave you

the salt instead of the sugar."

"It's not fair!" said Arthur.

"My presents never turn out right.

My lamp would not stand.

My cookies are like rocks.

Nothing I make is any good."

He began to cry.

"You cut the cookies right,"
said Violet. "They *look* nice."
"You know what?" said Norman.
"My mother makes play-clay
with flour and salt and water.
These cookies are made of
flour and salt and water.

Arthur has baked clay cookies—
clay angels and bells and stars
and Christmas trees and Santas."
"I made a clay paperweight,"
said Violet.
"I am painting it blue."

Arthur stopped crying.

He wiped his eyes and blew his nose.

He drank all of his hot chocolate.

Then he thought for a while.

"Maybe I could still use my cookies," said Arthur.

"Maybe I could paint them all different colors."

"You can't eat clay cookies even if they are different colors," said Wilma.

"They would not be for eating," said Arthur. "They can be Christmas tree ornaments! Mother and Father can hang them on the tree.

They will have my present
every Christmas for a long time."

Arthur blew his nose again.

Then he got out his paints

and the tape and some hooks.

Everyone watched Arthur

paint the cookies.

He painted the angels pink
and the Christmas trees green.
He painted the bells gold
and the stars silver.
Then Arthur taped a hook
to the top of each cookie.

Wilma said,

"I am going to paint my Santa
and put it on our tree."

"I am going to paint
my reindeer too," said Violet.

"I like Arthur's ornaments
better than the ones in the store."

"They are not bad," said Norman.

"They are kind of nice."

"Yes," said Arthur.

"They are kind of nice.

I made a good present
after all."

Everyone had more hot chocolate.

This time,

Arthur put *two* marshmallows

in each cup.

And when they were done,

they all helped

clean up the kitchen.

But Arthur wrapped
his Christmas present
for Mother and Father
by himself.

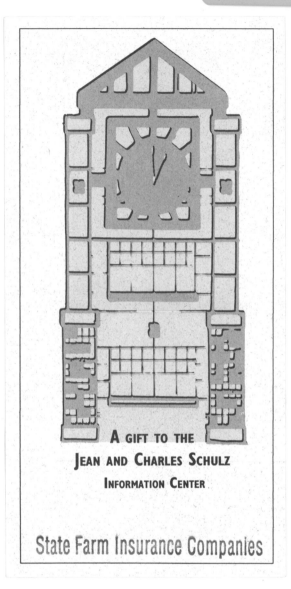

A GIFT TO THE
JEAN AND CHARLES SCHULZ
INFORMATION CENTER

State Farm Insurance Companies